STRIP easy

by Christiane Meunier

Chitra
Publications

2 Public Avenue • Montrose, PA 18801-1220
www.QuiltTownUSA.com • (800) 628-8244

Introduction

For me making quilts is very much about self-expression. Most of the time I don't really know what is being expressed before the quilt is finished.

I feel my way through it. On one hand, I find it hard to be intuitive when I have to carefully measure every step of the way. On the other hand, I find that the structure of the traditional block and the connection to generations of quilters gives me a sense of safety that makes it possible for me to go beyond my comfort zone. It makes it easier for me to get in touch with my emotions. Working with strips is my way of staying within the safety net of the quilting tradition without having to get too entangled in the mathematical part of it.

I find that when using strips that are an even width, (like the first four quilts in this book) and by alternating

Chitra Publications
2 Public Avenue
Montrose, Pennsylvania 18801-1220

Second Printing 2005

Library of Congress Cataloging-in-Publication Data

Meunier, Christiane, 1952-
    Strip easy / by Christiane Meunier.
        p. cm.
    ISBN 1-885588-61-5 (pbk.)
    1.   Patchwork--Patterns. I. Title.
            TT835.M48723 2004
            746.46'041--dc22
            2004011553

Edited by: Debra Feece
Illustrations: Brenda Pytlik
Book Design: InCahoots Design, Ashland, Oregon
Photography: Van Zandbergen Photography,
                    Brackney, Pennsylvania

Our Mission Statement:
We publish quality quilting magazines and books that recognize, promote, and inspire self-expression.
We are dedicated to serving our customers with respect, kindness, and efficiency.

www.QuiltTownUSA.com

or graduating light, medium, and dark fabrics, I can easily create a quilt with very clean directional lines and a depth of field that adds a mysterious quality. Look at "Demeter's Well" or "One World Over;" you'll see that for both of these quilts, while the surface design is very clean, a third dimension is being evoked — inside the well or behind the barn raising.

Irregular strips are a lot of fun to play with. I find it very freeing to cut strips without measuring. It is about creating a larger piece of fabric. Combined with the use of traditional blocks, this technique gives the quilt a lot of rich texture and movement. Look at "Sisterhood;" it is made using large Drunkards Path blocks. Using a single piece of fabric, this quilt would be quite dull, as would "Black Butterfly."

I hope you enjoy making "Strip-easy" quilts as much as I do. I hope they give you an easy way to express the deeper part of yourself and that they will become a great mirror into your inner emotions.

With all my love,

Christiane

Contents

Demeter's Well

Quilt Size: 61" x 78-3/4"

Materials

- Light, medium, and dark fabrics totaling at least 6 yards
- 2 1/4 yards blue/green print
- 3/4 yard darkest print for the binding
- 4 1/2 yards backing fabric
- 65" x 81" piece of batting

Cutting

Dimensions include a 1/4" seam allowance. Separate the strips into 5 piles grating from light to dark.

- Cut 20:   2" x 44" strips, darkest prints
- Cut 20:   2" x 44" strips, dark prints
- Cut 20:   1 1/2" x 44" strips, medium prints
- Cut 20:   2" x 44" strips, light prints
- Cut 20:   2" x 44" strips, lightest prints
- Cut 8:   2 1/2" x 44" strips, darkest print, for the binding

From the blue/green print:

- Cut 2:   5" x 74" lengthwise strips
- Cut 2:   5" x 63" lengthwise strips
- Cut 2:   7 1/2" x 74" lengthwise strips

Directions

1. Sew one strip from each pile into a panel, grating them from lightest to darkest, as shown. Make 20. Press all seam allowances toward the darker fabrics.

2. Using the 60° line on your ruler, cut 6 triangles from each panel, as shown.

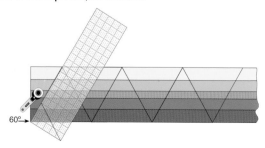

3. Cut one of the 7 1/2" x 74" blue/green strips as follows for pieces A and AR:

- Straighten the edge.

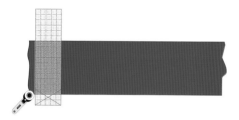

- Starting at least 1" from the edge, place the 60° line of the ruler along the bottom of the strip, as shown, and cut piece A.

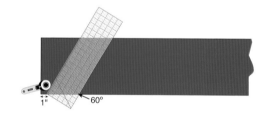

- Starting at least 1" from the top edge of the previous cut, straighten the fabric, as shown.

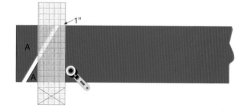

- Starting at least 1" from the cut, line up the 60° line of the ruler with the bottom edge of the strip, as shown, and cut piece AR.

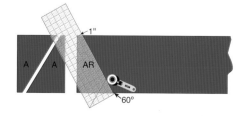

4

(continued on page 9)

Demeter in Greek mythology is the nurturing mother. At one point in the story, she sits by a well to grieve the loss of her daughter, Persephone, who was abducted by Hades, the lord of the underworld. I made this quilt to honor all the generations of mothers who have grieved the loss of their children's innocence.

(Quilted by Shelly Knapp)

Moving Out

Quilt Size: 57" square

Materials

- 1/4 yard each of 20 assorted prints
- 2 yards dark blue print
- 3 1/2 yards backing fabric
- 60" square of batting

Cutting

Dimensions include a 1/4" seam allowance.

- Cut 36: 2 1/2" x 44" strips, assorted prints in 18 matching pairs
- Cut 24: 1 1/2" x 44" strips, assorted prints in 12 matching pairs
- Cut 8: 7 5/8" x 23" lengthwise strips, dark blue print
- Cut 6: 2 1/2" x 44" strips, dark blue print, for the binding

Directions

1. Sew three 2 1/2" x 44" strips and two 1 1/2" x 44" strips together alternately, to make a panel, as shown. Make 2 using the same strips in the same positions. Make a total of 6 matching pairs of panels.

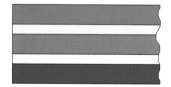

2. Cut four 8" squares from each panel.

3. Cut 4 matching squares in half diagonally from upper left to lower right. Cut 4 squares in half diagonally from lower left to upper right. Separate the triangles into piles according to direction. Repeat for each set of matching squares.

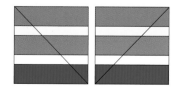

4. Join 2 matching triangles, one from each pile, to make a square. Make 4.

5. Sew the squares together to make the quilt center.

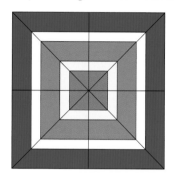

6. Sew 2 matching triangles, one from each pile, to make a large triangle. Make 8. Set 4 aside.

7. Sew the large triangles to the sides of the quilt center.

8. Join 2 matching triangles, one from each pile to make a large triangle. Make 8.

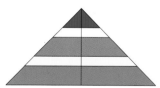

9. Sew 2 large matching triangles together, to make a large triangle. Make 4.

(continued on page 8)

This quilt is about our ability to move through very difficult situations in a beautiful and graceful way when we make sure that we do not lose our connection to our heart. (Quilted by Barbara Tidus • Pattern: Medallion)

10. Sew large triangles to the sides of the quilt.

11. Select 4 sets of 8 matching triangles from each pile. From each set of matching triangles make the following units:

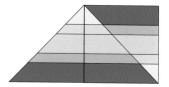

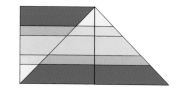

12. Referring to the Assembly Diagram, place the quilt center on a design wall. Arrange the units around the center. Place the large triangles set aside in Step 6 in the middle of each side.

13. Sew the pieces into sections, as shown, and join the sections.

14. Place two 7 5/8" x 23" dark blue print strips right sides together. Trim the left edge at a 45° angle, as shown. Repeat for the remaining dark blue strips.

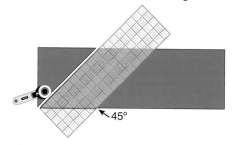

15. Select 8 matching triangles, 4 from each pile. Sew a triangle to each trimmed strip. Join the strips to make a border. Make 4.

16. Sew the borders to opposite sides of the quilt, matching the center seams.

17. Carefully trim the corners at a 45° angle.

18. Repeat steps 8 and 9 with the remaining triangles.

19. Sew large corner triangle.

20. Finish the quilt as described in the *General Directions,* using the 2 1/2" x 40" dark blue print strips for the binding.

- Continue cutting as before to make 6 A and 6 AR's as shown.

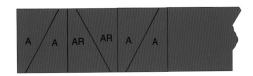

4. Continue cutting from the same blue/green strips as follows for pieces B and BR:

   - Start at least 5" from the beginning of the strip and place the 60° line of the ruler along the bottom edge of the strip, as shown and cut a B.

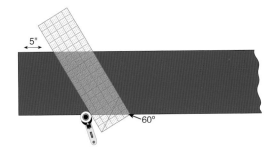

   - Continue cutting in the same manner to make 2 B's and 2 BR's.

5. Cut 14 triangles out of the other 7 1/2" x 74" blue/green strip.

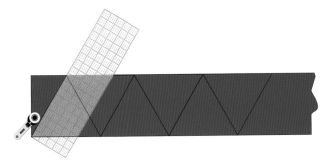

Assembly

1. Lay out the pieced triangles in 8 vertical rows. Place the blue/green B and BR pieces in the first and last rows. Place the A and AR pieces at the ends of the rows.

2. Sew the triangles into vertical rows. Join the rows.

3. Trim the top and bottom edges, leaving a 1/4" seam allowance.

4. Measure the length of the quilt. Trim the 5" x 74" blue/green strips to that measurement. Sew them to the sides of the quilt.

5. Measure the width of the quilt, including the borders. Trim the 5" x 63" blue/green strips to that measurement. Sew them to the top and bottom of the quilt.

6. Finish the quilt as described in the *General Directions*, using the 2 1/2" x 44" black print strips for the binding.

One World Over

Quilt Size: 90" square ❖ Block Size: 11 1/2" square

Materials

- 1/4 yard (9" x 44") each of 42 assorted light, medium and dark fabrics, for the blocks
- 36 assorted off white and yellow scraps, each at least 4" square, totaling 1/2 yard
- 4 yards black
- 93" square of batting
- 7 3/4 yards backing

Cutting

Dimensions include a 1/4" seam allowance.

From each light, medium and dark:

- Cut 1:   3" x 44" strip
- Cut 1:   2" x 44" strip
- Cut 1:   1 1/4" x 44" strip

NOTE: Separate the strips into groups by width.

Also:

- Cut 36:   3 1/2" squares, off white or yellow, then cut them in quarters diagonally to yield 144 small triangles
- Cut 4:   2 1/2" x 94" strips, black, for the binding
- Cut 4:   1 3/4" x 92" strips, black, for the outer border
- Cut 7:   1 3/4" x 78 1/4" strips, black, for the sashing
- Cut 42:   1 3/4" x 12" strips, black, for the sashing
- Cut 20:   B, black
- Cut 2:   13" squares, black; then cut them in half diagonally to yield 4 corner triangles

Directions

1. Make templates A and B (including seam allowance) from the pattern on page 21.
2. Staying within one color family and shading from light to dark, stitch one 3" strip to a 2" strip along their length. Stitch a 1 1/4" strip to the 2" strip to make a strip set. Make 42.

3. Place template A on one end of one strip set. Place a straight ruler on the slanted edge of the template. Using a rotary cutter, cut trapezoids from the panels, flipping the template and ruler after every cut. Cut 4 trapezoids from each panel, for a total of 168 trapezoids. Set 24 aside for the border.

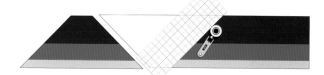

4. Center and stitch a small off white or yellow triangle on the top (shortest side) of a trapezoid. (You may want to lay out your blocks prior to adding the top triangle in order to know where to stitch the yellow or white triangles to make a solid center square.) Press the seam allowance toward the trapezoid. Trim the triangle even with the sides of the trapezoid. Make 144.

5. Sort the triangles into matching pairs and stitch them into half-blocks. Make 72.

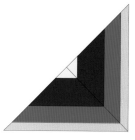

6. Stitch a light half-block to a dark half-block. Make 36.

(continued on page 21)

I love this quilt!...It is hanging in my living room and I don't get tired of looking at it. It speaks to me of the fact that there is more to life than what meets the eyes. And being reminded of that makes my life easier. (Quilted by Terri Birchard)

Weaving Around the Block

Quilt Size: 73 1/2" x 87 1/2" ❖ Block Size: 14" square

Materials

- 1 1/4 yards each of 3 dark red and brown prints

  NOTE: For variety, use a medium print for some blocks.

- 2 1/4 yards light print
- 2 3/4 yards green print
- 5 1/4 yards backing fabric
- 78" x 92" piece of batting

Cutting

Dimensions include a 1/4" seam allowance.

- Cut 72:   1 1/2" x 44" strips, assorted red and brown prints
- Cut 2:   1 1/2" x 2 1/2" rectangles, red print
- Cut 48:   1 1/2" x 44" strips, light print
- Cut 20:   4 1/2" squares, green print
- Cut 4:   2 1/2" squares, green print
- Cut 2:   3" x 77" lengthwise strips, green print
- Cut 2:   3" x 67" lengthwise strips, green print
- Cut 4:   4 3/4" x 81" lengthwise strips, green print
- Cut 4:   2 1/2" x 88" lengthwise strips, green print, for the binding

Directions

1. Sew two 1 1/2" x 44" light strips and three 1 1/2" x 44" same dark strips together alternately to make a panel. Make 24. Set 4 aside.

2. Cut one 14 1/2" section, two 9 1/2" sections, and one 4 1/2" section from each of the remaining 19 panels.

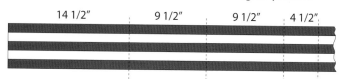

3. Sew a 4 1/2" section to a 4 1/2" green print square, as shown. Make 20.

4. Sew a 9 1/2" section to each unit, as shown.

5. Sew a 9 1/2" section to each unit, as shown.

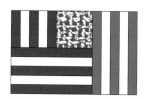

6. Sew a 14 1/2" section to the remaining side of each unit.

7. Cut fifty-four 2 1/2" sections from the panels you set aside.

Assembly

1. Referring to the photo, lay out the blocks in 5 rows of 4. Sew the blocks into rows and join the rows.

2. Measure the length of the quilt. Trim the 3" x 77" green print strips to that measurement. Sew them to the long sides of the quilt.

(continued on page 20)

This was just a great idea...there was no deep emotional meaning attached to it...
it worked...it looks like weaves. It looks complicated, but it is so easy and fast...
a real deal! (Quilted by Terri Birchard • Pattern: Log Cabin)

Black Butterfly

Quilt Size: 48" x 64" ❖ Block Size: 8" square

Materials

- Fat quarter (18" x 22") each of 10 assorted bright prints and batiks
- Fat quarter each of 10 assorted dark prints and batiks
- 3/4 yard black print for the binding
- 4 1/2 yards backing fabric
- 52" x 68" piece of batting
- Template plastic or heavy cardboard

Cutting

Dimensions include a 1/4" seam allowance.

- Cut 7 or 8: 1 1/2"-wide to 3"-wide strips, each 22" in length, from each fat quarter.

NOTE: Cut the strips an uneven width from one end to the other.

- Cut 7: 2 1/2" x 44" strips, black print, for the binding

Directions

1. Separate the 22"-long strips into brights and darks.

2. Sew 4 to 6 strips, right sides together along their length, to make a pieced panel at least 10" wide. Make 12 bright panels and 12 dark panels.

3. Cut 2 squares from each panel approximately 10" on a side. Make a total of 24 bright and 24 dark squares.

4. Make a cutting template from stiff cardboard or template plastic in the following way: cut a 10" square from the template material. Draw a gentle curve diagonally from corner to corner. Cut the template along the line. (You'll be cutting 2 templates but only using one.)

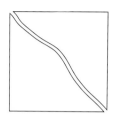

5. Stack a bright pieced square on a dark pieced square, right sides up with the strips running horizontally. Place the selected template on top, and trace the curved edge of the template. Remove the template and cut through both blocks along the curved line. If you've used very heavy cardboard, you may eliminate the tracing step and use a small rotary cutter to carefully cut along the curved edge of the template.

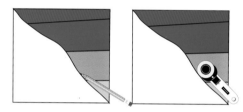

6. Lay out the 4 halves in 2 pairs, placing each bright half with an opposing dark half, as shown. Sew them together to make 2 blocks.

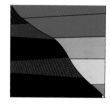

7. Make 23 more pairs of blocks in the same manner.

8. Trim the blocks to 8 1/2" square.

Assembly

1. Referring to the photo, lay out the blocks in 8 rows of 6. Sew the blocks into rows and join the rows.

2. Finish the quilt as described in the *General Directions*, using the 2 1/2" x 44" black print strips for the binding.

Black Butterfly

I made this quilt during a painful period of deep transformation. It is my version of "with that much manure, there's got to be a pony in there!"

(Quilted by Joanie Keith • Pattern: Half-square Triangle)

Quilt Size: 62" x 80" ❖ Block Size: 15" square

Materials

- 28 fat quarters assorted prints
- 2 1/8 yards blue print
- 4 yards backing fabric
- 66" x 84" piece of batting

Cutting

The pattern for Triangle A (on page 20) includes a 1/4" seam allowance as do all dimensions given. Flip the half-pattern on the dashed line to make a complete pattern. Make a template from the pattern. Cut the binding strips before cutting other strips from the fat quarters.

- Cut 17: 2 1/2" x 20" strips, assorted prints, for the binding
- Cut approximately 200: 20"-long strips in various widths from 1 1/2" to 3", assorted prints

NOTE: Cut the strips an uneven width from one end to the other.

- Cut 2: 4 1/2" x 64" lengthwise strips, blue print
- Cut 2: 2 1/2" x 72" lengthwise strips, blue print
- Cut 2: 2 1/2" x 38" lengthwise strips, blue print
- Cut 4: 7 1/2" x 29" strips, blue print
- Cut 4: 7 1/2" x 15" strips, blue print
- Cut 12: 2 1/2" x 15 1/2" strips, blue print

Directions

1. Sew 20" strips together to make a panel at least 7" wide. Make 24.

2. Using template A, cut 2 triangles from each of 12 panels, as shown. Set aside the leftover panel end sections.

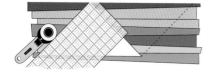

3. Cut 2 triangles from each of the remaining panels, as shown. Set aside the leftover panel end sections.

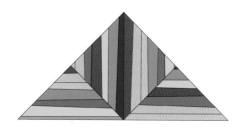

4. Sew 2 triangles together to make a large pieced triangle, as shown. Make 48.

5. Sew 2 large pieced triangles together to make a half block. Make 12.

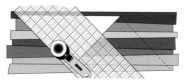

6. Join two half blocks to make a block. Make 4. Trim them to 15 1/2" square. Set them aside.

(continued on page 18)

In some Latin-American cultures, an on-point square is a symbol to meditate on to get in touch with the divine. It might be why I always loved that design. It does feel to me like a "more than meets the eye" design. This quilt is by far the most challenging quilt in this book. It works in a mysterious way. (Thanks to pattern writer Debra Feece, it's not as mysterious as it was when I made it!)...and it works.

(Quilted by Shelly Knapp • Pattern: Square-in-a-square)

7. Lay out one of the remaining large pieced triangles. Measure 4 1/4" from the long edge and cut to yield one pieced triangle and one trapezoid. Cut the remaining large pieced triangles in the same manner.

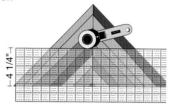

8. Mix up the pieces and sew a pieced triangle to a trapezoid to make a large pieced triangle. Trim to even the edges. Make 24.

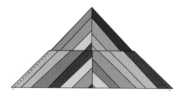

9. Sew 2 large pieced triangles together, matching the seams, to make a half block. Make 12. Set 6 aside.

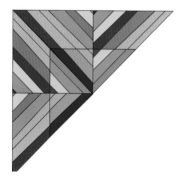

10. Sew 2 half blocks together to make a block. Make 3. Trim them to 15 1/2" square.

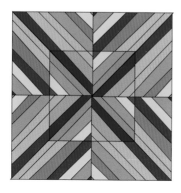

11. Lay out a half block and measure 11 1/8" from the bottom edge along the vertical seam. Make a mark. Trim the 2 short sides of the triangle at a 45° angle from that mark to the bottom edge. Repeat for each remaining half block.

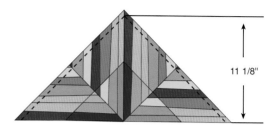

12. Referring to the *Assembly Diagram*, lay out the blocks and half blocks.

13. Place the 2 1/2" x 15 1/2" blue print strips between the blocks and the remaining 2 1/2"-wide blue print strips between the rows. Sew the blocks and short strips into rows. Join the rows and long strips.

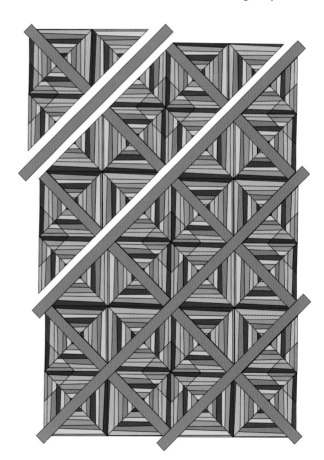

14. Trim the ends of the blue strips to square the quilt.

Diamond Self

For the border:

1. Join 2 of the end sections left over in Step 2 to make a square. Trim 2 adjacent edges of the square at a right angle, as shown. Make 12.

2. Sew 2 squares together, placing the trimmed edges in the center and at the bottom. Measure 6 3/4" from the bottom edge along the vertical seam. Make a mark. Trim the 2 short sides of the triangle at a 45° angle from the mark to the bottom edge. Make 6.

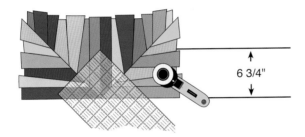

3. Lay out a 7 1/2" x 29" blue print strip, right side up. Make a mark near the end of the strip on the bottom edge. Measure 26 7/8" from the mark and make another mark. Stack the 7 1/2" x 29" blue print strips right sides up, placing the marked strip on the top.

4. Cut the ends of the strips at a 45° angle, starting at the marks, as shown. You will have 4 trapezoids.

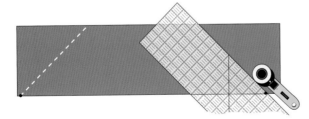

5. Lay out a 7 1/2" x 15" blue print strip, wrong side up. Make a mark near the end of the strip on the top edge. Place the marked strip on another 7 1/2" x 15" strip, right sides together. Stack 2 pairs in this manner. Stack the pairs together with the marked strip on top.

6. Cut the end of the strip at a 45° angle, starting at the mark, as shown. These are end sections.

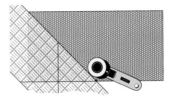

7. Sew a triangle to a blue print trapezoid. Trim the trapezoids even with the edge of the triangle. Make 2.

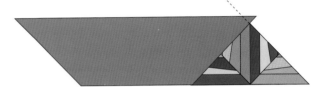

8. Sew a triangle to an end section and trim, as shown.

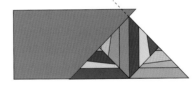

9. Lay out the units and an end unit, as shown. Sew them together to make a border. Make 2.

10. Sew the borders to the long sides of the quilt, matching the pieced sections. Trim the ends of the borders.

11. Measure the width of the quilt. Trim the 4 1/2" x 64" blue print strips to that measurement. Sew them to the top and bottom of the quilt.

12. Finish the quilt as described in the *General Directions*, using the 2 1/2"-wide assorted strips for the binding.

TRIANGLE A
DIAMOND SELF

Flip on the dashed line to make a complete pattern.

Weaving Around the Block continued from page 12

Weaving Around the Block continued from page 12

3. Measure the width of the quilt, including the borders. Trim the 3" x 67" green print strips to that measurement. Sew them to the top and bottom of the quilt.

4. Sew fifteen 2 1/2" sections together, end to end, to make a border. Make 2.

5. Sew the borders to the long sides of the quilt.

6. Sew twelve 2 1/2" sections together, end to end, to make a border. Make 2. Sew a 1 1/2" x 2 1/2" red rectangle to the light end of each border.

7. Sew a 2 1/2" green print square to each end of the borders.

8. Sew the borders to the top and bottom of the quilt.

9. Trim two 4 3/4" x 81" green print strips to fit the quilt's length. Sew them to the sides of the quilt.

10. Trim the remaining 4 3/4" x 81" green print strips to fit the quilt's width and sew them to the top and bottom of the quilt.

11. Finish the quilt as described in the *General Directions*, using the 2 1/2" x 81" green print strips for the binding.

Assembly

1. Referring to the quilt photo, lay out the blocks to achieve the setting you desire.

2. Stitch 6 blocks with seven 1 3/4" x 12" black sashing strips into a row. Make 6 rows.

3. Lay out the rows with seven 1 3/4" x 78 1/4" black sashing strips. Stitch them together to make the quilt center.

4. From the remaining 24 colored trapezoids, stitch 6 together with 5 black B's to make a border row. Make 4.

5. Referring to the quilt photo, stitch a border row to each side of the quilt center, aligning the border units with the blocks.

6. Stitch a corner triangle to each corner. Trim the outer edges of the triangles to square the quilt.

7. Measure the length of the quilt. Trim two 1 3/4" x 92" black strips to that measurement. Sew them to opposite sides of the quilt.

8. Measure the width of the quilt and trim the remaining 1 3/4" x 92" black strips to that measurement. Sew them to the quilt.

9. Finish the quilt according to the *General Directions,* using the 2 1/2" x 94" black strips for the binding.

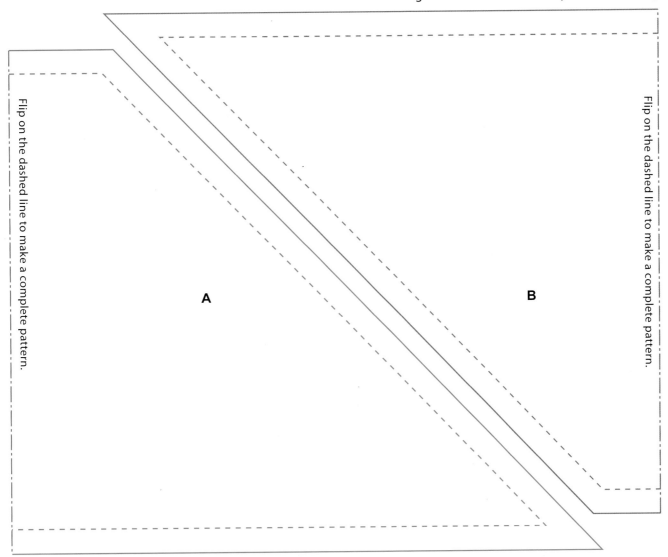

Flip on the dashed line to make a complete pattern.

Flip on the dashed line to make a complete pattern.

A

B

Quilt Size: 85 1/2" x 54" ❖ Block Size: 4 1/2" square

Materials

- Assorted dark prints totaling at least 5 yards
- Assorted light prints totaling at least 3 1/4 yards
- 3/4 yard dark print for the binding
- 5 yards backing fabric
- 90" x 58" piece of batting

Cutting

Dimensions include a 1/4" seam allowance.

- Cut the dark and light prints into 22"-long strips of various widths from 2" to 3".

NOTE: Cut the strips an uneven width from one end to the other.

- Cut 8: 2 1/2" x 44" strips, dark print, for the binding

Directions

1. Sew assorted dark strips into a pieced panel that's approximately 6 1/2" to 7 1/2" in width. Make approximately 45.

2. Make approximately 28 light panels in the same manner.

3. Cut 1 1/2" to 3"-wide sections from the pieced panels. These sections should also vary in width from one end to the other. Separate the light and dark sections into separate piles.

4. Lay out 3 dark sections cut from different panels. Sew them into a free-form Nine Patch block. Make 142 dark blocks and 86 light blocks.

5. Using a rotary cutter and ruler, cut the blocks in half diagonally.

6. Pair a light half-block with a dark half-block and sew them together. Make 172.

7. Make 56 dark blocks using the remaining half blocks.

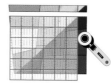

8. Aligning the 45° angle line of a square ruler with the diagonal seam, trim 2 sides of the block. Turn the block and trim the remaining sides to make a block that's 5" square.

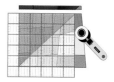

Assembly

1. Lay out the blocks in 12 rows of 19. Sew the blocks into rows and join the rows.

2. Finish the quilt as described in the *General Directions*, using the 2 1/2" x 44" dark print strips for the binding.

A few years ago I moved from Pennsylvania to Oregon. Becoming part of a new community and learning to navigate in a different culture (East Coast/ West Coast) was a rich and wonderful adventure and at that time I felt like I was in a labyrinth making one "wrong" turn after another.

(Quilted by Joanie Keith • Pattern: Nine Patch)

Prayer Wheel

Quilt Size: 64" x 76" ❖ Block Size: 12" square

Materials

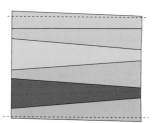

- 20 fat quarters (18" x 22") assorted bright prints
- Assorted light prints totaling at least 1 1/2 yards
- 1/3 yard light print for the border
- 2 yards teal print
- 4 1/2 yards backing fabric
- 68" x 80" piece of batting

Cutting

Dimensions include a 1/4" seam allowance.

- Cut 22"-long strips in various widths from 2" to 3", assorted bright prints.

NOTE: Cut the strips an uneven width from one end to the other.

- Cut 80:   B, assorted light prints
- Cut 6:   1" x 44" strips, light print
- Cut 4:   4 1/2" x 70" lengthwise strips, teal print
- Cut 5:   2 1/2" x 70" lengthwise strips, teal print, for the binding
- Cut 4:   2 1/2" x 62" lengthwise strips, teal print

Directions

1. Sew 22" bright strips together to make a panel at least 13" wide. Make 20.

2. Using a ruler and template pattern on page 30, cut 4 A's from each panel, as shown, in either of the following ways:

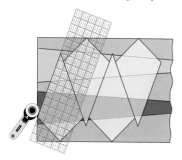
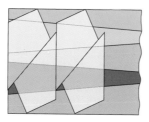

3. Straighten the remaining pieces of the panels in the following way.

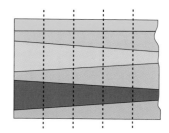

4. Cut twenty 2" sections from the remaining pieces of the panels. Set them aside.

5. Lay out 4 A's and 4 light B's, as shown. Sew the pieces into pairs, then join the pairs to make a block. Make 20.

Assembly

1. Lay out the blocks in 5 rows of 4. Sew the blocks into rows and join the rows.

2. Measure the length of the quilt. Trim two 2 1/2" x 62" teal strips to that measurement. Sew them to the long sides of the quilt.

3. Measure the width of the quilt, including the borders. Trim the remaining 2 1/2" x 62" teal strips to that measurement. Sew them to the top and bottom of the quilt.

4. Sew 2" pieced sections together, end to end, to make a border at least 65" long. Make 2.

(continued on page 30)

Tibetan Prayer Wheels (called Mani wheels by the Tibetans) are devices for spreading spiritual blessings and well-being. As I was driving across the country a few years ago following the Oregon Trail, I felt that each turn of the emigrant wagon's wheel must have been the result of a prayer. Now feels like a good time to make prayer wheels. (Quilted by Terri Birchard • Pattern: Rocky Road to Kansas)

Sisterhood

Quilt Size: 50" x 70" ❖ Block Size: 10" square

Materials

- 12 fat quarters of assorted warm-color hand-dyed and batik fabrics
- 18 fat quarters of assorted cool-color hand-dyed and batik fabrics
- 3 1/4 yards backing fabric
- 54" x 74" piece of batting
- 3/4 yard blue print for the binding

Cutting

Dimensions include a 1/4" seam allowance. From each warm- and cool-color hand-dyed and batik fabric:

- Cut 22" strips of various widths from 1 1/2" to 3" wide

NOTE: Cut the strips an uneven width from one end to the other.

Also:

- Cut 7: 2 1/2" x 44" strips, blue print, for the binding.

Directions

1. Separate the strips into warm and cool colors.

2. Sew 6 or more warm-color strips into a pieced panel at least 11" wide. Make 7.

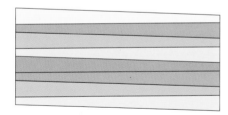

3. Make 18 panels in the same manner, using cool-color strips.

4. Using the templates on page 29, cut B's and D's from the warm-color panels, paying careful attention to direction, as shown. Cut 28 B's and 25 D's.

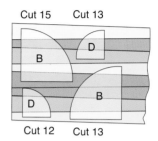

5. Cut thirty-four 10 1/2" squares and four 5 1/2" squares from the cool-color panels.

6. Align the corner of template A on the lower right corner of a 10 1/2" square and trace the curved edge. Cut on the line. Stitch a warm-color B to the square to make a Block A. (See step-by-step instructions on page 31.) Make 6.

Block A • Make 6

7. Make 7 block B's in the same manner placing the quarter circle in the lower left corner.

Block B • Make 7

8. Cut a C from the upper left corner of a 10 1/2" square. Sew a D to the square to make Block C. Make 4.

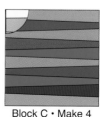

Block C • Make 4

26

(continued on page 28)

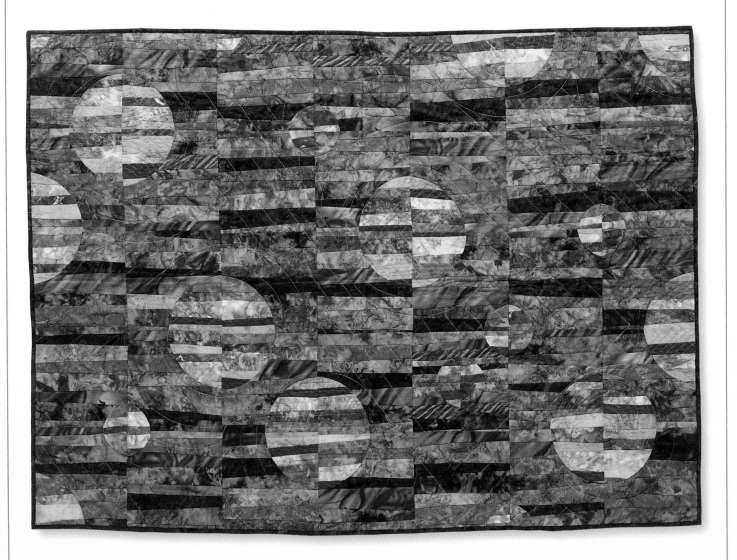

For me this quilt shows what it feels like to be part of a community of women where everyone is given space to be herself, where every member is accepted and loved just the way she is. (Quilted by Joanie Keith • Pattern: Drunkard's Path)

9. Following the block diagrams, make the blocks
indicated.

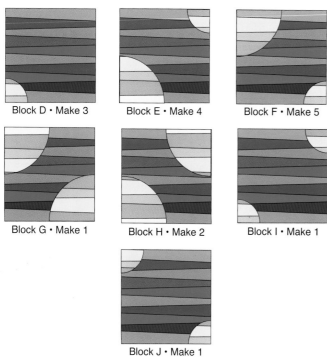

Block D • Make 3   Block E • Make 4   Block F • Make 5

Block G • Make 1   Block H • Make 2   Block I • Make 1

Block J • Make 1

10. Make 4 blocks, as shown, using the 5 1/2" squares
and remaining D's. Sew the squares together to
make a block.

Assembly

1. Referring to the Assembly Diagram, lay out the blocks
in 7 rows of 5.

2. Sew the blocks into rows and join the rows.

3. Finish the quilt as described in the *General Directions,*
using the 2 1/2" x 44" blue print strips for the binding.

Sisterhood

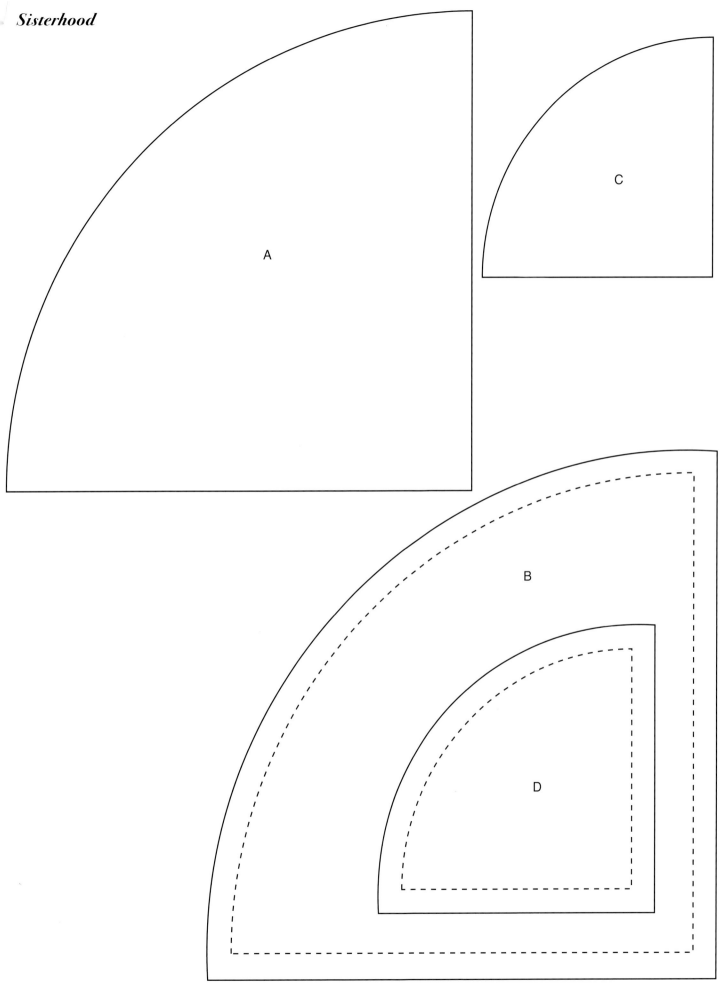

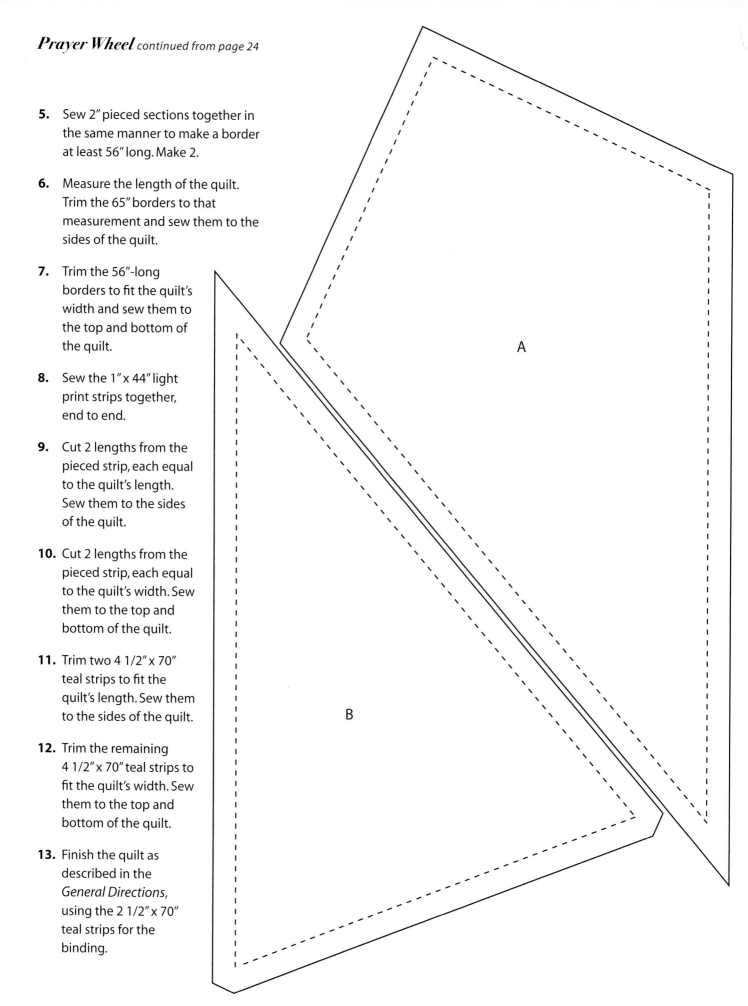

5. Sew 2" pieced sections together in the same manner to make a border at least 56" long. Make 2.

6. Measure the length of the quilt. Trim the 65" borders to that measurement and sew them to the sides of the quilt.

7. Trim the 56"-long borders to fit the quilt's width and sew them to the top and bottom of the quilt.

8. Sew the 1" x 44" light print strips together, end to end.

9. Cut 2 lengths from the pieced strip, each equal to the quilt's length. Sew them to the sides of the quilt.

10. Cut 2 lengths from the pieced strip, each equal to the quilt's width. Sew them to the top and bottom of the quilt.

11. Trim two 4 1/2" x 70" teal strips to fit the quilt's length. Sew them to the sides of the quilt.

12. Trim the remaining 4 1/2" x 70" teal strips to fit the quilt's width. Sew them to the top and bottom of the quilt.

13. Finish the quilt as described in the *General Directions*, using the 2 1/2" x 70" teal strips for the binding.

A

B

1. Make a template for each piece. Mark templates.

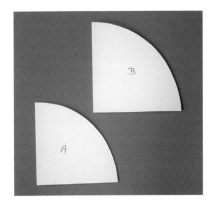

2. Cut out a background piece and a quarter circle as directed in the pattern on page 26.

3. Fold each piece in half, pinch fold to make a crease and mark with a pencil on the wrong side of the fabric.

4. Fold each piece in quarters, pinch to make a crease and mark with a pencil on the wrong side of the fabric.

5. Place the background piece on the quarter circle, right sides together, and pin center.

6. Pin each end being careful to line up the edges.

7. Pin at each quarter mark.

8. Sew with the background piece on top. Remove the pins as you go and keep the edges aligned.

9. Press the seam allowance toward the quarter circle to finish the block.

10. Finished block.

About the patterns

Read through the pattern directions before cutting fabric. Yardage requirements are based on fabric with a useable width of 44". Pattern directions are given in step-by-step order. If you are sending your quilt to a professional machine quilter, consult the quilter regarding the necessary batting and backing size for your quilt.

Fabrics

I suggest using 100% cotton. Wash fabric in warm water with mild detergent. Do not use fabric softener. Dry fabric on a warm-to-hot setting. Press with a hot dry iron to remove any wrinkles.

Templates

Template patterns are full size and unless otherwise noted, include a 1/4" seam allowance. The solid line is the cutting line; the dashed line is the stitching line. Place a sheet of firm, clear template plastic over the patterns and trace the cutting line and/or stitching line for each one. Templates for machine piecing include a seam allowance.

Piecing

For machine piecing, sew 12 stitches per inch, exactly 1/4" from the edge of the fabric. To make accurate piecing easier, mark the throat plate with a piece of tape 1/4" to the right of the point where the needle pierces the fabric.

Pressing

Press with a dry iron. Press seam allowances toward the darker of the two pieces whenever possible. Otherwise, trim away 1/16" from the darker seam allowance to prevent it from shadowing through. Press abutting seams in opposite directions. Press all blocks, sashings, and borders before assembling the quilt top.

Finishing your quilt
Binding

Cut the binding strips with the grain for straight-edge quilts. To make 1/2" finished binding, cut 2 1/2"-wide strips. Sew strips together with diagonal seams; trim and press seam allowance open.

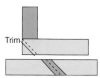

Fold the strip in half lengthwise, wrong side in, and press. Position the strip on the right side of the quilt top, aligning the raw edges of the binding with the edge of the quilt top. Leaving 6" of the binding strip free and beginning a few inches from one corner, stitch the binding to the quilt with a 1/4" seam allowance measuring from the raw edge of the quilt top. When you reach a corner, stop stitching 1/4" from the edge of the quilt top and backstitch. Clip the threads and remove the quilt from the machine. Fold the binding up and away from the quilt, forming a 45° angle, as shown.

Keeping the angled fold secure, fold the binding back down. This fold should be even with the edge of the quilt top. Begin stitching at the fold.

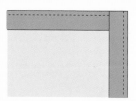

Continue stitching around the quilt in this manner to within 6" of the starting point. To finish, fold both strips back along the edge of the quilt so that the folded edges meet about 3" from both lines of the stitching and the binding lies flat on the quilt. Finger press to crease the folds. Measure the width of the folded binding. Cut the strips that distance beyond the folds. (In this case 1 1/4" beyond the folds.)

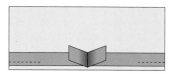

Open both strips and place the ends at right angles to each other, right sides together. Fold the bulk of the quilt out of your way. Join the strips with a diagonal seam as shown.

Trim the seam allowance to 1/4" and press it open. Refold the strip wrong side in. Place the binding flat against the quilt, and finish stitching it to the quilt. Trim excess batting and backing so that the binding edge will be filled with batting when you fold the binding to the back of the quilt. Blindstitch the binding to the back, covering the seamline.

Remove visible markings. Make a label that includes your name, the date the quilt was completed, and any other pertinent information, and stitch it to the back of your quilt.